u

SALT & FAITH

Apostle Marguerite Breedy-Haynes

Rehoboth
Barbados

USING SALT & FAITH

Rehoboth books may be ordered through Amazon.com and other booksellers.

Breedy-Haynes, Marguerite
Using Salt & Faith

ISBN-13: **978-1547130061**
ISBN-10: **1547130067**

Printed in the United States of America

I dedicate this booklet to Jesus Christ my Lord and Savior who is the lover of my soul and to the precious Holy Spirit who continues to walk with me and teaches me all things

Foreword

It is of the upmost importance that God's people come into the knowledge that He has given us in His words. This booklet **"Using Salt & Faith"** unravels key revelation points about the use of salt in our everyday lives which many have failed to see. God is the creator of salt and we must not allow the enemy to use what God has given us for his evil purposes while we, the ones for whom it was meant lie down and play dead.

It is time that we utilize the tools that God has given us, one of which is salt and begin to chase the enemy out of our lives, homes, schools, children and family. Our eyes have been opened and I pray that those who take this book in their hands would not just read it but put it into practice so that they can experience the victory that God has intended for them in Jesus Name.

HOW I FOUND OUT THE POWER OF SALT

Five years ago, I was struggling as a minister and there were many things that I did not understand, it looked like evil had surrounded me. There was many evil activities I saw at my home and I could not understand why these things were happening. I would go to bed and see snakes by the door and front house.

I had to protect my children in my dreams. One day I was sitting in the patio and I saw a rat came through the door and when I looked everywhere there was none and the Lord opened my eyes to the spirit realm. Then my husband began to behaving in ways he should not. I knew then that there was evil trying to destroy the lives of me and my children.

I moved everything and there was no trace of what I saw come through the door. It was not until I went to bed and had a vision where the Lord spoke to me through a woman and said "Daughter my people are being destroyed because of lack of knowledge." He told me to take Kosher salt and pray over it. He told me that a house has four corners and to put it in all four corners of the house and pray over it with the name of Jesus.

He told me that evil had surrounded my home and that the kingdom of darkness was using people to bring trouble to my house and that I should use the salt to clean up my home. I was troubled because I knew nothing about this and when I asked ministers about it, they had no knowledge of the use of salt.

When I realized that they had no knowledge of what I was saying I knew that God had given me a revelation that no one had. I began to activate salt and faith using the salt and the problems I had in my home disappeared completely. I truly believe that if many of us would seek God there are things that He would give us the knowledge to eradicate what is happening in our homes and communities.

It is up to us to open our minds and hearts to hear what He is saying to us in the season. It is His desire to show us unsearchable things that we do not know (Jeremiah 33:3). Are we willing to open our hearts and minds to remove the spirit of complacency to hear Him?

1. THE SEMITIC PEOPLE USED SALT

The Bible tells us in Genesis that everyone on earth was drowned except for Noah and his family and that all humanity are descended from his three sons, Shem, Ham, and Japheth. The Semite people descended from Shem, the eldest of the three sons of Noah. When the Semitic people left their homes to travel, they would put Salt around the windows and doors. If a thief planned to enter, he would not cross over the Salt for fear of swift judgment coming to him or his family. They understood the power of Salt activated by faith, the Salt Covenant.

If we would understand the power of salt, many of our problems would be resolved a long time ago. Salt is one of the most powerful tools that can be used by a believer with their faith in action. Salt can be used to remove demonic entities and witchcraft that is sent to destroy a person

It can be used to clean a plot of land and praying to Jesus using your faith to activate the salt can be dangerous. You can even curse a plot of salt with salt. Salt is such a powerful tool and if believers understood the power of salt, deliverance would have come to many already.

2. THE SALT COVENANT

Hosea 4:6

6 my people are destroyed from lack of knowledge. "Because you have rejected knowledge, I also reject you as my priests; because you have ignored the law of your God, I also will ignore your children.

Proverbs 4:7

7 The beginning of wisdom is this: Get wisdom. Though it cost all you have, get understanding.

SALT REQUIRED

In ancient Judaism God required the Levites (priests) to use Salt in every Sacrifice.

And every oblation of your meat offering shall you season with salt: neither shall you allow the salt of the covenant of your God to be lacking from your meal offering: with all your offerings you shall offer salt. Leviticus 2:13

All the heave offerings of the holy things offered...it is a covenant of salt forever...Numbers 18:19

For everyone shall be salted with fire, and every sacrifice shall be salted with fire. Salt is good; but if the salt have lost its saltiness, with what will you season it? Have salt in yourselves, and have peace one with another. Mark 9:49-50

You are the salt of the earth. Matthew 5:13

This little mineral must be very important in the eyes of God for Him to put such importance on it. The Salt Covenant is a Lasting Covenant between God and the Priesthood. A few of the natural reasons God may have chosen to use Salt is because of its Purification and Preservation properties. However, there are much deeper reasons, we probably yet are not aware of.

What is Salt made of? (1) Hydrochloric Acid (2) Sodium Hydroxide Base. The Word of God says that, we are to have Salt within ourselves. Spiritually speaking there must be a proper balance of acid and base. Many of God's people are out of balance, they are either too **Acidic (religious)** or **too Basic (liberal).**

A false balance is a disgrace, but a just weight is His delight. Proverbs 11:1 **Legalism produces self-righteousness, and liberalism produces unrighteousness.** Have Salt in yourselves.

All warm-blooded animals and humans need Salt to stay healthy. 3% of the Oceans weight is Salt. 12% of the Salt Lakes weight is Salt, and nearly 30% of the Dead Sea weight is Salt. The weight percentages are no coincidence, these numbers (3, 12, 30) all have prophetic relevance for our day.

Salt was at one time the currency for ancient Ethiopia and Tibet. Our English word Salary was derived from the Latin term Salarium, which was the Salt portion issued to Roman Soldiers. Salt was their money. **Salt has always been very important in every culture.**

3. SPIRITUAL USES OF SALT

Salt has been used in Religious Rites from the beginning of time. The Greeks, Romans, Africans, Hebrews, Druids and Christians all use Salt in certain rituals. For many religions, Salt is the Salvation Covenant. Salt is a symbol of Wisdom (Light), and a symbol of Friendship.

Salt is blessed and used with water for baptism, also for blessing the home and animals by the Catholic Church. The Salt must first be exorcised (prayed over to drive out impurities and negative energies). Then it can be used for many purposes such as:

14

Healing - 2 Kings 2 The waters are very polluted and causing death. The prophet Elisha uses Salt to heal the waters.

Purification - Ezekiel 16:4 Newborns were rubbed with it. It was believed to rid the child of negative influences, evil spirits, and to harden the skin.

Judgment/Curses - Hebrew tradition teaches us that when the angels came to the house of Lot, that his wife refused to feed them (using salt). We will later find out the importance of using salt with guests. She was afraid of the reproach from the people of Sodom. Do you remember Lot's wife? She was turned her into a pillar of Salt.

Abimelech cursed the soil of Shechem with Salt.- Judge 9:45

Even the ungodly know how to use salt because of understanding the power that lies in it - Japanese Sumo wrestlers throw blessed Salt in the ring before wrestling to drive out evil spirits. Just in case the opponent has "fixed" the match by using spiritual powers, the Salt will break the curse.

4. ANCIENT CUSTOMS & UNSPOKEN COVENANTS

Did you ever wonder why Jews (Judeans) did not eat with Gentiles? Some New Testament references are in Acts 10, Galatians 2 - Why New Testament Christians were told not to keep company (eat) with sinners? 1 Corinthians 5 Salt was always on the table, not just for seasoning. The understanding of Salt was common among all the nations of the East and Middle

East. **To eat Salt with someone meant that you were entering into in a covenant relationship with him or her. You partook of their hospitality; therefore, you became obligated to them. It also meant that you partook of whatever spirit they were of.**

A practicing Jewish person would never eat with a Gentile, because they did not want to be obligated to look out for their best interest. Therefore, they could remain superior in their thinking. Other reasons are, they did not want to be exposed to non-kosher foods or foods offered to idols.

In Ezra 4:14 the word maintenance is used in the KJV Bible "Now because we have maintenance from the king's palace, and it was not meet for us to see the king's dishonor, therefore have we sent and certified the king;.."

These men had eaten with Artaxerxes, the king of Persia (Iran); they were therefore obligated to warn the king if they knew of something that might bring harm to him or his kingdom. Therefore, they advised him not to allow the Jews to rebuild the Temple; it was a threat to all false religions. Do you understand the power of the Salt that people all over that region clearly understood? **It was the Salt Covenant** - and Unspoken Covenant Relationship. Can you imagine how authentic relationships would be today, if people understood what actually takes place on this level when we break bread? There is an energetic exchange and soul ties are made at some levels.

In certain countries today, many of the covenants or contracts are done with Salt. In business or personal dealings, after making promises, they sprinkle Salt on bread and say, **the Salt is**

between us, and then eat it. They feel that just as Salt can preserve life; it can also destroy, if contracts are broken.

JESUS

Jesus last message/plea to the Laodicean Church Age was, I am knocking outside your door, let me come in to eat (Salt Covenant) with you. Let me be responsible for taking care of you, protecting and blessing you. I want to be obligated to you. Revelation 3:20

This was a people that felt they had everything, and had it all together. They were prosperous, and very satisfied with the old time religion. There was no need for seeking God anymore. They were very much like our society. Can't you hear the plea in His Voice? **"I want to sup with you; I want you to spend time with me. Allow me to care for you."** Listen to His Voice.

BLESSED SALT

Keep in mind, that the Kingdom of God is not in word only, but in demonstration and power. Just as anointing oil is a symbol and has no power of itself, and must be used in faith; so it is with the Salt. It can be activated and programmed by your words or thoughts to assist in many things.

Expect healings, miracles, blessings, for your family, animals, home or vehicle; you must have something in mind as you use it in faith.

5. THE DAVIDIC SALT COVENANT

Three thousand years ago, God made a covenant with the House of David, it was later called the Davidic Covenant, and this was the 7th Biblical Covenant. It was revealed that this was a **Salt Covenant.**

After God observed David's unrestrained, radical praise and worship when bringing the Ark of the Covenant back to Jerusalem, and seeing his desire to build a house for Him; God made a covenant with David. In 2 Samuel 7 it is outlined, but Salt is not mentioned. You will have to go to 2 Chronicles 13:5

"And Abijah set the battle in array with an army of valiant men of war, even four hundred thousand chosen men: Jeroboam also set the battle in array against him with eight hundred thousand chosen men, being mighty men of valor. And Abijah stood up upon mount Zemaraim, which is in mount Ephraim, and said, Hear me, thou Jeroboam, and all Israel; Ought ye not to know that the Lord God of Israel gave the kingdom over Israel to David forever, even to him and to his sons by a COVENANT OF SALT?" 2 Chronicles 13: 3-5

King Jeroboam of Israel with his 800,000 chosen men of war goes out against King Abijah of Judah and his 400,000 men of war. Something very strange happens in the midst of the battle. Abijah stands up on Mount Zemaraim (meaning= dual fleece-double witness), which is in the hill country of Ephraim (meaning= doubly fruitful-double portion), and reminds Jeroboam of the Covenant of Salt with the house of David. Verse 3-5

In essence, Abijah says, Give it up Jeroboam, there is no way you can win. Although you have twice the amount of men, you are stronger; all odds are against us in the natural. However, there is one little thing I should remind you of, with heaven and earth as my witnesses, as I stand in the place of double portion: **the Salt Covenant** that God made with the house of David.

You can just see Abijah holding up a rock of salt and crumbling it, as the wind blew it in Jeroboam's face. Sometimes you have to remind the adversary, whatever your enemy appears to be. It could be overwhelming Bills, Foreclosure, Health issues, Relationship issues, Depression, Fear, Condemnation, Guilt, or Spiritual Weaknesses. Hold up your Salt and remind the adversary, yourself or situation of the Salt Covenant.

Arise in consciousness NOW. Get to the place of double portion; face the problem. **There is no way you can lose.** Your Father/God does not break promises (covenants), whatever outcome, you WIN. **YOU WIN!** No weapon formed against you can prosper. In the natural, all odds may appear to be against you for your specific situation or need. The Salt is on your side and at a moment's notice, things can change. Favor, Favor, Favor is yours. The scales are tipped in your favor says the Lord.

(Jeroboam's army was destroyed that day, and Jeroboam never recovered. They could not prevail against the Salt Covenant). While holding your salt, take a selah moment and see victory for every situation that might be before you.

This is a clue in the Old Testament foreshadowing the Change in the Priesthood. Somebody with faith, knowledge and boldness had to stand up and declare it. Abijah had received a revelation about the Salt. Do you have it yet? **Are you awake yet??!!**

As you may remember David was anointed to be king, however, he partook of the priest's bread. The law said the priest could not be king and the king could not be priest, but we see David experiencing both in part. Psalms 110 is a prophetic psalm of the king-priest ministry, foreshadowing Jesus the son (descendant) of David that would be a priest after the order of Melchizedek. This also foreshadowed a people that would realize the Salt Covenant, stand up in the realization of double-portion, fullness, and declare it. Nothing happens until it comes out of your mouth, your words are what create reality or the illusion. The Creator used "words" to create all that you see and cannot see.

Melchizedek was King of Salem, and Priest of the Most High God (El Elyon). David was king of Jerusalem and partook of the priest's bread, not fully realizing the king-priest ministry. Jesus was called king of Jerusalem.

"...Jerusalem; for it is the city of the great King." Matthew 5:35

Jesus was also called a priest.

"The old priesthood of Aaron perpetuated itself automatically, father to son, without explicit confirmation by God. But then God intervened and called this new, permanent priesthood into being with an added promise: God gave his word; he won't take it back: You're the permanent priest. This makes Jesus the guarantee of a far better way between us and God one that really works! A new covenant." Hebrews. 7:21-22 Message Bible

It would take a King - Priest Ministry to raise humanity up. Someone in touch with humanity and in touch with the Divine.

6. SALT COVENANT CONTRACT & AGREEMENT

Covenant, a contract, agreement, or promise between at least two parties. Growing up I remember hearing my mother, uncles and others saying, **my word is my bond.** I had no idea what that meant as a child. Later my mother explained to me the importance of keeping my word, being a person of integrity.

The Salt Covenant was an everlasting covenant between God and the Levitical Aaronic Priesthood.

"All the heave offerings of the holy things, which the children of Israel offer to the Lord, I have given to you and your sons and daughters with you as an ordinance forever; it is a

covenant of salt forever before the Lord with you and your descendants with you." Numbers 18:19

After about 500 years, something happened. We know that God does not lie, cannot lie, for He is Truth. God does not change His mind back and forth, He is not unstable. However, there was a problem with the Priesthood, therefore, it had to be changed.

If, therefore, perfection were by the Levitical priesthood. What further need was there that another priest should rise after the order of Melchizedek, and not after the order of Aaron? For the priesthood being changed, there is, made of necessity a change also of the law. Our Lord sprang out of Judah, of which tribe Moses spoke nothing concerning priesthood... which is made after the power of an Endless life...And they (Aaronic priesthood), truly were many priest, because they were not allowed to continue by reason of death. But this man, because he continues ever, has an Unchangeable priesthood. Hebrews 7:11-24

7. THE ORDER OF MELCHIZEDEK

There is not a whole lot written about this Melchizedek (Jesus Christ). References are made to him in Judaism and Christianity as an eternal being with no human ancestry. He descended to this planet. Judaism and Christianity sprung from the blessings Abraham received from Melchizedek, the righteous king of peace.

Melchizedek is considered the first teacher of the Most High God (El Elyon). He is called a King and Priest of the Most High God, who brings forth bread and wine (elements for coming into a union, communion, which produces life, immortality) to Abraham.

David speaks about an Order, also the writer of Hebrews records it. That means there were more than one. Melchizedek is immortal, no ending of days, and he is the leader of this Order. This is a Priesthood, which ministers from both the Seen and Unseen realms. Who are they? From the Seen realm, those who are overcoming and identify with Melchizedek; preaching life and immortality. From the Unseen realm, the many that are among us which have existed and ministered on the physical and spiritual planes throughout the ages, they yet minister. We call them angels. They are not limited to one group of people; they transcend race, religion and time.

The Order of Melchizedek is not limited to planet Earth or our solar system; it's universal and trans-dimensional. Are you beginning to understand the power of the Salt Covenant and how a specific element called Salt was used to seal the deal?

God compares the Aaronic Priesthood, which was always dying, with the Melchizedek Priesthood that yet lives. David was aware of it over 700 years after Abraham. The writer of Hebrews said that there was a witness that Melchizedek was yet alive, nearly 3000 years after he was first mentioned.

"Here mortal men receive tithes, but there he receives them, of whom **it is witnessed that he lives.**" Hebrews 7:8

Somebody had witnessed Melchizedek decades after Jesus' ascension. We are talking immortality, never physically dying and its connection with the Salt Covenant.

The Davidic Salt Covenant is a promise and prophecy that as God restores the house (tabernacle) of David, people would stop dying. Isn't that what Jesus taught us, that if we would truly believe with our entire being, we would never die? In addition, he demonstrated it by dying in our place and overcoming death. Jesus Is Alive!

"Verily, verily, I say unto you, He that hears my word, and believes on him that sent me, has everlasting life, and shall not come into condemnation; but is passed from death unto life." John 5:24 KJV

Melchizedek is the Priesthood that ministers life and immortality. Those of us who are overcoming can stand in the high place of double portion and remind death of the Salt Covenant, and death will become powerless. The revelation of the Salt Covenant (Davidic Covenant) reaches way beyond sacrifices, ancient customs, and rituals. **This is the Covenant of Life and Immortality,** which points to Melchizedek, a kingdom of priests (you and I).

Immortality is living in and out from the eternal moment (Now), and choosing to take this physical form to a higher form, escaping what is called physical death. This is the highest form of immortality, the higher calling that we should be pressing toward the mark for, as Apostle Paul did. This is the full realization of the Salt Covenant in us.

Appreciation

I would like to extend a very heartfelt thank you, first to God the Father, Son and Holy Spirit who directed me in writing this book. To my immediate family for their constant support. To Apostle Anthony Greaves, Evangelist Cora Beckles, Miss. Valarie Deane, Dr. Philip Corbin, Pastor Ron Hercules and Prophetess Debbie Isaac who saw the anointing upon my life when no one else saw it.

I am very grateful to Pastor Cheryl Harewood for believing in my calling and I would like to extend my sincerest gratitude to Anthony Devonish, Reverend Michelle Marshall, Reverend Wasim Worrell, Reverend Kerrie Worrell, Reverend Waldron, Minister Waldron, Evangelist Arlene, Minister Maria Clarke and the members of the congregation for standing with me in ministry.

I also want to extend a special thank you to Reverend Kerrie Worrell who took the time to proofread my entire book before it was published.

About The Author

Apostle Marguerite Breedy-Haynes was born in St. Lucia to one Barbadian parent and one St. Lucian parent and is the seventh of sixteen children. She lived in Barbados since childhood and is married with three children.

Saved by Jesus who visited her in a vision, she was taken to hell, and there she was given a mandate by God not to let anyone go to that place. She then gave her life completely over to Him and was anointed as an End Time Prophet. Her ministry began by giving tracts on the streets of Barbados for over 3 years until God promoted her.

Saving The Lost At Any Cost, End Time Ministries' was started at her house and has now become an international ministry with branches based in Barbados, South Carolina, St. Lucia and several others which are being birthed around the world. Hundreds came to her from all over Barbados. Their lives were changed through the deliverance of the Word of God, many were healed and demons were cast out.

As an End Time Prophet, she was called to preach the gospel of the second coming of the Lord Jesus Christ. She has travelled the world ministering in various churches and crusades, teaching and admonishing others to live holy lives before God. She is known for not compromising the Word of God and believes in living what she preaches. Her desire is to win souls for the end times and to snatch God's children from the hands of the enemy.

I pray that this booklet has been a blessing to you. For more information on the author, her ministry and her books, please contact us or visit us at:

Telephone: (246) 437-8418

Website: www.SavingTheLostAtAnyCost.org
Address: Saving The Lost At Any Cost End Time Ministries
        Pasture Road, Mapp Hill
        St. Michael
        Barbados
        West Indies

Facebook:https://www.facebook.com/savingthelostinternational/

Twitter: https://twitter.com/savingthelost1

Medium: https://medium.com/@savingthelost

Email: savingthelost@live.com
Instagram: Savingthelostatanycost

Journal